Abbey Theatre presents

Kicking a Dead Horse

By Sam Shepard

First performance at the Abbey Theatre, Peacock Stage, Dublin

on 12 March 2007

The Abbey Theatre greatfully acknowledges the financial support
from the Arts Council/an Chomhairle Ealaíon

ABBEY THEATRE

join us

Become a Friend or Member of the
Abbey from as little as €125 and enjoy
a host of benefits. Be among the first to
hear about what's coming up, book your
tickets ahead of the crowd and receive
invitations to a wide range of events.

visit
www.abbeytheatre.ie
for details

Kicking a Dead Horse

By Sam Shepard

The production runs without an interval

CAST

Hobart Struther	**Stephen Rea**
Young Woman	**Joanne Crawford**
Director	**Sam Shepard**
Set Design	**Brien Vahey**
Lighting Design	**John Comiskey**
Costume Design	**Joan Bergin**
Voice Director	**Andrea Ainsworth**
Dialect Coach	**Brendan Gunn**
Assistant Director	**Wayne Jordan**
Company Stage Manager	**Brendan McLoughlin**
Deputy Stage Manager	**Elizabeth Gerhardy**
Assistant Stage Manager	**Róisin Coyle**
Hair and Make-up	**Patsy Giles**
Photography	**Ros Kavanagh**
Graphic Design	**Red Dog**
Horse Makers:	
Sculptors	**Padraig McGoran, John O'Connor**
Mechanism	**Shadow Creations**
Assistants	**Tony Doody, Rory Doyle**
Model maker	**Mike McDuff**

Special thanks to Peter Stampfel

The Abbey Theatre wishes to thank RTÉ Television for their support of new writing.

Please note that the text of the play which appears in this volume may be changed during the rehearsal process and appear in a slightly altered form in performance.

SAM SHEPARD WRITER AND DIRECTOR

Sam Shepard had his first New York plays, *Cowboys* and *The Rock Garden*, produced by Theatre Genesis in 1963. For several seasons, he worked with Off-Off-Broadway theatre groups including La MaMa and Caffe Cino. Eleven of his plays have won Obie Awards including *Chicago* and *Icarus's Mother* (1965); *Red Cross* and *La Turista* (1966); *Forensic and the Navigators* and *Melodrama Play* (1967); *The Tooth of Crime* (1972); *Action* (1974) and *Curse of the Starving Class* (1976). He was awarded a Pulitzer Prize as well as an Obie Award for his play *Buried Child* (1979). The critically acclaimed production of *True West*, starring John Malkovich and Gary Sinise opened in New York in 1984. *Fool for Love* (1982) received the Obie for Best Play as well as for Direction. *A Lie of the Mind* (1985) won the New York Drama Critics' Circle Award in 1986 and the 1986 Outer Critics' Circle Award for Outstanding New Play. *States of Shock* premiered at the American Place Theatre in 1991 and a new play, *Simpatico* transferred to the Royal Court Theatre after its premiere in 1994 at the New York Shakespeare Festival. *When the World was Green (Chef's Fable)*, was written with his long-time collaborator, Joseph Chaikin and commissioned by Seven Stages in Atlanta, premiered at the Olympic Arts Festival. A revived *Buried Child* under the direction of Gary Sinise opened on Broadway in April 1996 and won a Tony Award nomination. Signature Theatre Company devoted its '96-'97 season to his work. *Eyes for Consuela* premiered at the Manhattan Theatre Club in 1998 and in 2000 *The Late Henry Moss* premiered at the Magic Theatre in San Francisco before opening in New York the following year. His latest play *The God of Hell* received its world premiere in New York during 2004, at the same time as Sam appeared in the New York premiere of Caryl Churchill's *A Number* at New York Theatre Workshop.

He wrote the screenplays for *Zabriskie Point*; Wim Wender's *Paris, Texas*; Robert Altman's *Fool for Love*, a film version of his play of the same title. As writer/director, he filmed *Far North* and *Silent Tongue* in 1988 and 1994 respectively. As an actor he has appeared in the films *Days of Heaven*, *Resurrection*, *Raggedy Man*, *The Right Stuff*, *Frances*, *Country*, *Fool for Love*, *Crimes of the Heart*, *Baby Boom*, *Steel Magnolias*, *Bright Angel*, *Defenseless*, *Voyager*, *Thunderheart*, *The Pelican Brief*, *Safe Passage*, *Hamlet* and *Don't Come Knocking*, also co-written with Wim Wenders.

In 1986, he was inducted into the American Academy of Arts and Letters. In 1992, he received the Gold Medal for Drama from the Academy and in 1994 he was inducted into the Theatre Hall of Fame.

STEPHEN REA HOBART STRUTHER

Began career at the Abbey Theatre before moving to London. His first theatre role in London was as Tommy Owens in *The Shadow of a Gunman* with Jack McGowran at the Mermaid Theatre. First directed by Sam Shepard in *Geography of a Horse Dreamer* at the Royal Court. Also acted in *Action* at the Royal Court and *Buried Child* and *Killer's Head* at the Hampstead Theatre and directed *Little Ocean* by Sam Shepard (also at the Hampstead). Worked extensively at the English National Theatre and the Royal Court where he worked with Samuel Beckett on *Endgame*.

He was a founder member of Field Day Theatre Company with Brian Friel.

Films include *Stuck, Sisters, Sixty Six, Till Death, V for Vendetta, Breakfast on Pluto, The River Queen, The Good Shepherd, Control, The Halo Effect, Ulysses, The I Inside, Evelyn, FearDotCom, The Musketeer, The End of the Affair, Guinevere, Still Crazy, In Dreams, The Butcher Boy, Fever Pitch, The Last of the High Kings, Trojan Eddie, Michael Collins, Between the Devil and the Deep Blue Sea, All Men Are Mortal, Prêt-a-Porter, Interview with a Vampire, Princess Caraboo, Angie, Bad Behaviour, The Crying Game, Life is Sweet, The Doctor and the Devils, The House, The Company of Wolves, Loose Connections* and *Angel*.

Stephen received an Oscar nomination and a Golden Globe nomination for *The Crying Game* and a Tony Award nomination for *Someone Who'll Watch Over Me*.

JOANNE CRAWFORD YOUNG WOMAN

This is Joanne's first appearance at the Abbey Theatre. She is from Derry and studied Theatre and Media Studies at University of Ulster, Coleraine. She also has a MA in Screenwriting from the National Film School Dun Laoghaire. Theatre credits include *Reflex* (Zulu Theatre), *One* (Pan Pan), *Master Shuttlefate* (Angel Exit), *Petty Sessions* (Red Kettle), *Can't Pay Won't Pay, Accidental Death of an Anarchist* and *Sister Mary Ignatius* (Blind Mirror). Film and television credits include *Pure Mule, Becoming Jane, Murphy's Law, The Clinic, Chosen, The Actors, Omagh, Maybe If You, The Hard Way, Too Many Sandwiches, The Puppet, The First Television* and *Jane by the Sea*.

BRIEN VAHEY SET DESIGNER

Brien is an Associate Artist with the Abbey Theatre. His work at the Abbey includes *A Number* which he recently designed and *A Whistle in the Dark* in 1986. He has worked extensively in Ireland, England and America. Theatre design includes *Three Sisters, The Hostage* (Druid), *An Ideal Husband* (Gate Theatre), *Antigone* (Field Day), *Three Days of Rain* (Rough Magic), *Sea Change* (Riverside Studios), *The Bells, A Doll's House* (Leicester Haymarket), *Cocktail Party, Portraits* (West End), *A Moon for the Misbegotten* (West End and Broadway), *The Shadow of a Gunman* (Broadway) and the opera, *La buona figliola* (Buxton Opera Festival). Television and film production design includes *Glenroe, Nighthawks, Fair City, Upwardly Mobile, On Home Ground, Making the Cut/DDU, Hell for Leather, Horse, After Midnight, The Battle of Inchion* and *Excalibur*. Brien is a graduate in Fine Art from the Dun Laoghaire School of Art. He won the DeVeres Prize at the RHA in 1998. His work has been widely exhibited in many galleries including the DeVeres Gallery, Solomon Gallery and the RHA. Brien is also a graduate of the Motley Theatre Design Course, Riverside Studios and has lectured in theatre design at the Motley Design Course, Bristol University, Suffolk College Ipswich and DIT, Mountjoy Square.

JOAN BERGIN COSTUME DESIGN

Joan is very pleased to return to the Abbey Theatre after a long absence. During the 1970s and 80s she was in-house designer for Focus Theatre and worked on many memorable plays such as *A Doll's House, Collier's Friday Night* and *A Month in the Country*. She also worked with Noel Pearson on many productions ranging from *The Pirates of Penzance* to Brian Friel's *Translations* on Broadway. Recent design work includes the *Pinter Season* and Billy Roche's *Poor Beast in the Rain* at the Gate and *Family Stories* and *Teja Verdes* with b*spoke. Her film career covers the Jim Sheridan greats, *My Left Foot, The Field, In the Name of the Father* and *The Boxer.* Recent work includes *Reign of Fire, Veronica Guerin* and *The Prestige*. Television highlights include Roddy Doyle's *Family* and *David Copperfield.* She has just completed work on *The Tudors*, a ten-part series for American Showtime.

JOHN COMISKEY LIGHTING DESIGNER

John's design work at the Abbey Theatre to date has been set, lighting
and video for *Hamlet*, set and lighting for *The Shape of Metal* (co-designed
with Alan Farquharson) and lighting for *The Drawer Boy* and *The Doctor's
Dilemma*. Other theatre work includes set and lighting designs for *Mermaids*
and *Hanging on by a Thread* (CoisCéim), *Only The Lonely* (Birmingham Rep)
and *Copenhagen* (Rough Magic) for which he won an Irish Times/ESB
Theatre Award. He has designed lighting for numerous theatre companies
including CoisCéim, Rough Magic, Prime Cut, Druid, Siamsa Tíre, Barabbas,
Galloglass, Operating Theatre (of which he was also an artistic director) and
two performance works by James Coleman. Work as director includes *The
Well* (Abhann Productions) and Gavin Friday's *Ich Liebe Dich*, both for the
Dublin Theatre Festival, and two years as production director of *Riverdance
- the Show* (Abhann Productions) worldwide. Film work includes directing the
award-winning *Hit and Run* and documentaries on the Dingle Wren's Day and
the Berlin years of Agnes Bernelle. Televised concerts include *Celtic Woman,
Brian Kennedy Live in Belfast* and *Ronan Tynan: The Impossible Dream* for PBS.
He was a television director with RTÉ for twelve years, where his credits
include *The Eurovision Song Contest 1995, Nighthawks, Today Tonight, popscene,
The Blackbird and the Bell, Fair City*, various *Telethons* and special events.
He is the curator of Ireland's first participation in the Prague Quadrennial
exhibition of theatre design and curated the *EXTR.acts* exhibition at the last
Dublin Theatre Festival.

WAYNE JORDAN ASSISTANT DIRECTOR

Wayne is the inaugural trainee director on a new mentoring programme
devised by the Abbey Theatre. His work at the Abbey Theatre includes
Assistant Director on *Julius Caesar, Alice Trilogy* written and directed by Tom
Murphy and *Portia Coughlan* by Marina Carr. He is a graduate of the Samuel
Beckett Centre, Trinity College Dublin. He is Artistic Director of Randolf SD
The Company. Wayne's own work has been seen primarily at the Project Arts
Centre where he most recently directed Federico Garcia Lorca's *The Public*
in The Cube with his own company and designed *Hedwig and The Angry Inch*
in the Space Upstairs for Making Strange. Other work includes *Eeeugh!topia,
The Illusion, The Drowned World* (Project Arts Centre), *Agememnon, Baal*
(Samuel Beckett Theatre) and *Crave* (Samuel Beckett Theatre and
Studiobuhne, Cologne).

AMHARCLANN NA MAINISTREACH

Ba iad W. B. Yeats agus Augusta Gregory a bhunaigh Amharclann na Mainistreach i 1903. Faoi phátrúnacht Annie Horniman, ceannaíodh áitreabh ar Sheansráid na Mainistreach agus ar an 27 Mí na Nollag 1904, osclaíodh doirse Amharclann na Mainistreach den chéad uair.

I dtosach, bhí Amharclann na Mainistreach faoi bhainistíocht National Theatre Society Ltd. Ar an 31 Eanáir 2006 díscaoileadh an chuideachta seo agus bunaíodh cuideachta nua, Abbey Theatre/ Amharclann na Mainistreach, a reáchtálann an amharclann anois. Níor tháinig athrú ar bheartas ealaíne Amharclann na Mainistreach go fóill agus cuimsíonn sé na spriocanna seo a leanas:

- chun dul i ngleic go gníomhach le agus léiriú a thabhairt ar shochaí na hÉireann

- chun cinntiú go bhfanfaidh an scríbhneoir agus ealaíontóir mar chuid lárnach d'Amharclainne na Mainistreach

- chun todhchaí iontach a chruthú do dhrámaíocht na hÉireann trí shaothair nua a choimisiúnú agus a léiriú

- chun an sméar mhullaigh de dhrámaíocht na hÉireann agus de dhrámaíocht an domhain a léiriú

- chun infeistiú a dhéanamh i bhforbairt ealaíontóirí Amharclainne Éireannacha.

I 1925, thug Saorstát nua na hÉireann fóirdheontas bliantúil neamhghnách d'Amharclann na Mainistreach, agus tháinig sí ina céad amharclann fóirdheonaithe stáit i dtíortha an Bhéarla. Coinníonn ar An Chomhairle Ealaíon, mar aon lenár gcuid cairde, ár mbaill, ár bpatrúin agus sibhse, ár lucht féachana, tacaíocht a thabhairt dár gcuid oibre.

I 1951, rinneadh damáiste do bhunfhoirgnimh Amharclann na Mainistreach de bharr dóiteáin. Athlonnaíodh Amharclann na Mainistreach go dtí Amharclann na Banríona. Cuig bliana déag cothrom an lae sin anonn, ar an 18 Iúil 1966, bhog Amharclann na Mainistreach foirgneamh nua, a dhear Michael Scott, ar an láthair chéanna.

I Meán Fómhair na bliana seo caite, d'fhógair an tUasal John O'Donoghue T.D., Aire Ealaíon, Spóirt agus Turasóireachta, gur ghac an Rialtas le comórtas deartha idirnáisiúnta do bhunláthair nua Amharclann na Mainistreach, a bheidh lonnaithe ar Dhuga Sheoirse i mBaile Átha Cliath.

Gabhaimid buíochas libh as bheith linn don chéad taibhiú domhanda de chuid Amharclann na Mainistreach de *Kicking a Dead Horse* le Sam Shepard. Tá súil againn go mbainfidh sibh sult as.

THE ABBEY THEATRE

The Abbey Theatre was founded in 1903 by W. B. Yeats and Lady Augusta Gregory. With patronage from Miss Annie Horniman, premises were purchased on Old Abbey Street and on 27 December 1904, the Abbey Theatre opened its doors for the first time.

The Abbey Theatre was originally managed by the National Theatre Society Limited. On 31 January 2006 this company was dissolved and a new company established, Abbey Theatre/Amharclann Na Mainistreach, which now runs the theatre. The artistic policy of the Abbey remains unchanged and incorporates the following ambitions:

- **to engage actively with and reflect Irish society**

- **to ensure that the writer and theatre-maker remain at the heart of the Abbey**

- **to create a great future for Irish theatre by commissioning and producing new work**

- **to produce both the best of Irish and world theatre**

- **to invest in the development of Irish theatre artists.**

In 1925, the Abbey Theatre was given an annual subsidy by the new Free State, becoming the first ever state-subsidised theatre in the English speaking world. The Arts Council of Ireland/An Chomhairle Ealaíon, along with our friends, members, patrons, benefactors and you, our audience, continues to support our work.

In 1951, the original buildings of the Abbey Theatre were damaged by fire. The Abbey re-located to the Queen's Theatre. Fifteen years to the day later, on 18 July 1966, the Abbey moved back to its current home, designed by Michael Scott, on the same site.

In September 2006, on behalf of the Irish Government, Mr. John O'Donoghue T.D., Minister for Arts, Sport and Tourism, announced that an international design competition will be held to create a new home for the Abbey, to be located at George's Dock in Dublin.

Thank you for joining us for the Abbey Theatre world premiere production of Sam Shepard's *Kicking a Dead Horse*. We hope you enjoy it.

STAFF AT THE ABBEY

Board
Bryan McMahon
(Chairman)
Catherine Byrne
Tom Hickey
Olwen Fouéré
Suzanne Kelly
Declan Kiberd
Dr. Jim Mountjoy
Eugene O'Brien
Maurice O'Connell
Lynne Parker
John Stapleton
Director
Fiach Mac Conghail
**Director of Finance and
Administration**
Declan Cantwell
Literary Director
Aideen Howard
**Director of
Public Affairs**
Catherine Carey
**Director of Technical
Services and Operations**
Tony Wakefield

ARTISTIC
Abbey Players
Des Cave
Aidan Kelly
Abbey Theatre
Trainee Director
Wayne Jordan
Anglo Irish Bank
Writer-in-Association
Enda Walsh
Associate Artists
David Gothard
Paul Keogan
Conall Morrison
Bairbre Ní Chaoimh
Brien Vahey
**Honorary Associate
Directors**
Vincent Dowling
Tomás MacAnna
Casting
Holly Ní Chiardha
Executive Office
Orla Mulligan
Voice
Andrea Ainsworth

**FINANCE AND
ADMINISTRATION**
Accounts
Ruth Cavanagh
Derek Garland
Suzanne Lowe
Paul Meagher
Pat O'Connell
Human Resources
Keira Matthews
Information Technology
Richard Bannister
Vincent Quinn

LITERARY
Archive
Mairéad Delaney
Mairéad Lynch
Literary
Aoife Habenicht
Temporary Senior Reader
Conall Quinn

Honorary Council
Kathleen Barrington Conor Bowman Siobhán Bourke Loretta Brennan Glucksman
Frank Cuneen Máiread Delaney Eugene Downes Paddy Duffy Clare Duginan
John Fairleigh Clive Geraghty Des Geraghty Eithne Healy Peadar Lamb John Lynch
Tomás MacAnna Patricia McBride Muriel McCarthy Paul Mercier Jimmy Murphy
Donal Nevin Edna O'Brien Niall O'Brien Ulick O'Connor John O'Mahony
Pat O'Reilly Peter Rose Michael J. Somers John Stapleton

PUBLIC AFFAIRS
Box Office
Des Byrne
Catherine Casey
David Clarke
Clare Downey
Anne Marie Doyle
Lorraine Hanna
Marie Claire Hoysted
Deborah McHugh
Iain Mullins
Front of House
John Baynes
Stephen Brennan
Ian Cooke
Claire Devregille
Con Doyle
Adam Doyle
Gavin Fowler
Philip Hanna
Michelle Gilmore
Michael McCormack
David McMenamy
Conor Matthews
Dominik Neinart
Brian O'Brien
Aine O'Sullivan
Magdalena Segieda
Noelle Tracey
Marketing
Janice McAdam
Jeanette
McGarry Keane
Lucy McKeever
Outreach/Education
Michelle Howe
Phil Kingston

Press and Publicity
Siobhán Colgan
Gemma Duke
Public Programme
Dominic Campbell
Reception
Donna Murphy
Stage Door
Patrick Whelan

TECHNICAL
Cleaning
Brian Kelly
Construction
Brian Comiskey
Kenneth Crowe
Mark Joseph Darley
John Kavanagh
Bart O'Farrell
Peter Rose
Lighting
Brian Fairbrother
Barry Madden
Kevin McFadden
Maintenance
Mick Doyle
Michael Loughnane
Production
Vanessa Fitz-Simon
Andy Keogh
Jon Woodley
Props
Stephen Molloy
Scenic Artists
Angie Benner
Jennifer Moonan
Brian Hegarty

Stage Management
Stephen Dempsey
Tara Furlong
Elizabeth Gerhardy
Audrey Hession
Aisling Mooney
John Stapleton
Stage Technicians
Pat Dillon
Gerry Doyle
John Finnegan
Patrick Gannon
Larry Jones
Fred Malone
Mick Russell
Sound
Eoin Byrne
Cormac Carroll
James Lindsey
Wardrobe
Sandra Gibney
Marian Kelly
Niamh Lunny
Vicky Miller

Abbey Theatre

Dublin

Spring 2007...

Abbey Stage

THE CAVALCADERS
By Billy Roche
Directed by Robin Lefevre
A wistful story of lives, loves and song
TUESDAY 10 APRIL - SATURDAY 19 MAY

THE CRUCIBLE
By Arthur Miller
Directed by Patrick Mason
Miller's great drama of the Salem witch trials
and political paranoia
SATURDAY 26 MAY - SATURDAY 7 JULY

Peacock Stage

SAVED
By Edward Bond
Directed by Jimmy Fay
A rare opportunity to see Bond's controversial masterpiece
FRIDAY 27 APRIL - SATURDAY 26 MAY

TERMINUS *World Premiere*
Written and directed by Mark O'Rowe
Hold tight as a night out turns fantastical
SATURDAY 9 JUNE - SATURDAY 7 JULY

Box Office: 01 87 87 222

www.abbeytheatre.ie

Sam Shepard
Kicking a Dead Horse

faber and faber

First published in 2007
by Faber and Faber Limited
3 Queen Square, London WC1N 3AU

Typeset by Country Setting, Kingsdown, Kent CT14 8ES
Printed in England by Bookmarque, Croydon, Surrey

All rights reserved
© Sam Shepard 2007

The right of Sam Shepard to be identified as author of
this work has been asserted in accordance with Section 77
of the Copyright, Designs and Patents Act 1988

All rights whatsoever in this work are strictly reserved.
Applications for permission for any use whatsoever including
performance rights must be made in advance, prior to any such
proposed use, for the United Kingdom to Josef Weinberger Plays,
12–14 Mortimer Street, London W1T 3JJ, or for the rest of
the world to Judy Boals, Inc., 307 West 38th St., #812,
New York, NY 10018

No performance may be given unless a licence
has first been obtained

*This book is sold subject to the condition that it shall not,
by way of trade or otherwise, be lent, resold, hired out or
otherwise circulated without the publisher's prior consent
in any form of binding or cover other than that in which
it is published and without a similar condition including
this condition being imposed on the subsequent purchaser*

A CIP record for this book
is available from the British Library

ISBN 978-0-571-23813-2

2 4 6 8 10 9 7 5 3 1

To Stephen Rea

Characters

Hobart Struther
mid-sixties

Young Woman

KICKING A DEAD HORSE

Scene: as the audience enters, the stage is entirely covered with a sky-blue silk sheet concealing irregular mounds. No special lighting and no music or sound effects of any kind. A blank white muslin scrim covers the side walls and the entire upstage wall, floor to ceiling. No light in scrim.

Once the audience settles, piano music begins: Dr John's 'A Closer Walk With Thee' (track 7 from the CD Dr John Plays Mac Rabenac). After the first short piano phrase, lights begin slowly to dim to black. This fade takes up the entire first, long verse of the song. Once the verse is completed and the lights have gone down to black, the scrim begins slowly to fill with a pale straw-coloured light reminiscent of wide open prairie at midday. As the second verse of the song unfolds and the lights are slowly rising with the music, the sky-blue silk sheet begins to be drawn back slowly towards the upstage wall, revealing a huge, dark pit downstage centre with mounds of fresh earth on either side of it. Directly upstage centre of the pit, on a slight rise, is a dead horse laid out on its side, spine to audience, neck and head sprawled out to stage right (from the actor's point of view), tail to stage left, all four legs pointed stiffly towards the upstage wall. There is no blood or sign of external injury. The dead horse should be as realistic as possible with no attempt to stylise or cartoon him in any way. In fact, it should actually be a dead horse.

Music fades out. Light is now full in scrim, giving the effect of a distant, endless horizon in flatlands. Silence for

*a short while then, from deep in the pit, the sound of a
shovel piercing earth followed by dirt flying up out of the
deep hole and landing on one of the mounds to the side.
This repeats four times in an exhausted rhythm, then a
man slowly emerges from the hole with a small camp
shovel. He climbs out of the pit, stabs his shovel into a
mound of earth and stares back down into the deep hole.*

*This is Hobart Struther, mid-sixties, rumpled white shirt,
no tie, sleeves rolled up to elbows, no hat, baggy dark
wool pants, plain boots for riding (*but* not *cowboy
boots), dark vest. There should be no attempt in his
costume to make him look like a 'cowboy'. In fact, he
should look more like an urban businessman who has
suddenly decided to rough it. He stares down into the pit
for a while, then upstage to the horse, then looks directly
at the audience, then back to the horse. Each of these
'looks' should be very distinct and deliberate in the mode
of the classic circus clown. He speaks to himself.*

Hobart Fucking horse. Goddamn.

> *He moves downstage right to one of the mounds of
> fresh earth, where a jumbled pile of equipment has
> been tossed: western saddle, horse-blanket, plain
> chaps, spurs, bridle, canteen, small duffle full of
> canned beans and pots and pans, small canvas tent in
> the old style, bedroll, rope, saddlebags and a brand
> new cream-coloured western hat. He starts sorting
> through all the gear, searching for a pair of large black
> binoculars in a case, talking to himself the whole
> while.*

(*Searching through gear.*) Of all the damn things – all the
things you can think of – the preparations – endless lists.
All the little details, right down to the can-opener and the
hunk of dental floss you throw in just for the heck of it –

All the forever thinking about it night and day – weighing the pros and cons – Last thing in the world that occurs to you is that the fucking horse is going to up and die on you! Just take a shit and roll over like a sack of bones.

Looks at audience, motions to horse.

Look at that! Dead! Deader than dirt. There he is – deader than dirt.

He finds the binoculars in the saddlebag, takes them out of their case and scans the horizon over the heads of the audience. He stands slowly, keeping binoculars to eyes. Talks to himself.

(*Scanning with binoculars.*) Now what? Nothing – Nowhere – Here I am – miles from nowhere. Only one day into it and bottomed out. Empty – Badlands – Horizon to horizon. No road – no car – no tiny house – no friendly Seven Eleven. Nada. Can't even track where I could have left the truck and trailer.

Takes binoculars away from eyes, stares out.

You ask yourself, how did this come to be? How is it possible? What wild and woolly part of the imagination dropped me here? Makes you wonder.

Looks upstage to horse, back to audience.

Fucking horse.

He hangs the binoculars round his neck by their strap and moves upstage towards horse, looking down into the pit as he skirts around it.

(*Approaching horse.*) Look at that. That's where he winds up. Snorts a chunk of oats down his pipe, straight into the lung, and wham! That's it. End of the day he's at the checkout counter. Gasping, wheezing like an old fart. Staggering – Dead. Barely even got started on the grand sojourn and he drops out from underneath me.

He kicks the horse in the belly, climbs up on top of it and sits on its ribcage, staring out towards the audience. He picks up the binoculars and scans again.

(*Sitting on horse, scanning.*) You try tracking it back in your raggedy mind to the original notion – the 'Eureka' of it. You remember the moment very clearly – how it came to you. Surprising: 'AUTHENTICITY'. That's what you come up with – the quest for 'AUTHENTICITY'. As though that were some kind of holy mission in itself.

Lowers binoculars, stares out.

How could that be? A haunted, ghostly idea to me any more. At least nowadays – days with age hanging on me like dry moss. Maybe, always, I don't know. Far back as I can remember. Some idea. Weighing the true against the false. Measuring, calculating – as though you were ever rock solid certain – as though you ever had the faintest clue.

Stops himself and listens to space. Pause. He stands on the ribcage, looking out; listens intently. He speaks to himself in an urgent whisper, punctuated by outbursts.

(*Standing on horse.*) And who is it exactly you're supposed to be appealing to now? Huh? Who? THERE'S NOBODY OUT THERE! Nobody. Do you see anybody?

Looks through binoculars.

No.

Do you hear anybody?

Lowers binoculars, listens.

No.

Do you have the least little sense of the presence of another being – listening? Listening –

Pause. Listens.

No. Nothing.

Then stop blathering on to yourself, for Christ's sake. What's the point?

Just the sound, I guess.

The sound?

Gives me the impression there's maybe someone else.

Don't make me sick. Your self is giving your own self the impression that there may be someone else?

Something like that.

You're one sick puppy.

Maybe so.

No question about it.

I need to verify certain things. Just for my own –

Be my guest. I'll be the last to get in your way.

No insult intended.

None taken.

All right – all right. Can't we just –

What?

Get along.

Hobart climbs down off the horse and crosses down
centre, in front of the pit. He talks directly and
confidentially to the audience.

(*To audience.*) All I can tell you is that I had become well
aware of my inexorable descent into a life in which, daily,
I was convinced I was not intended to be living. This is
in the style of the classic narrative. Bear with me. Things
will change. It's going to be a long, rough and rocky
road. I'm not sure what voice to use. What voice suits the
predicament. What – predicament I'm actually – It's – not
clear – but hopefully – as things roll along – hopefully –

He begins to stroll back and forth, extreme downstage,
continuing to address the audience.

(*Strolling.*) Long-story-short, it must have been some
other poor fool's destiny I had been assigned to because
I couldn't recognise it in any way, shape or form as my
own. Not one drop. Not even the simplest act, like
turning a doorknob or opening the mailbox or addressing
the doorman by name. Doorman? Oh, yes, I had become
quite the big-ass success. No question about that. Quite
the bigshot on the block. But somewhere along the trail
the thrill of the kill had eluded me. The ecstasy of power –
and now there was a kind of constant hankering for
actuality. Hankering – How else can you put it? The sense
of being inside my own skin. That's what I missed. That's
what I missed more than anything else in this world.

Pause.

How could you lose something like that?

Something shifts in him: a different query. He begins to
question himself and forgets about the audience.

(*To himself*.) Are we supposed to reach out now and somehow walk a mile in your sorry shoes? Now that you've got yourself into this jam? What is the appeal you're making exactly? You're not an immigrant, are you?

A what?

Immigrant.

Why should that be?

You sound funny. Suspicious.

Funny?

Foreign.

I don't know. Maybe it's you. Maybe it's the way you're hearing it.

Don't try to put it off on me, now.

I'm not.

Are you the son of an immigrant, maybe?

Probably so. What's the point?

The son of the son of an immigrant? Twice removed?

Twice?

One of those white barbarians Benjamin Franklin brought over to protect us from the Appalachian wilderness?

Absolutely not!

Then what's your story? Why beat around the bush?

Hobart stops. Turns to audience directly.

(*To audience.*) 'AUTHENTICITY'.

Pause, then continues to audience:

The little conundrum mounted slowly to a frantic state of crisis. I was running out of time. Birthdays flying by. I could see it coming. I sat down with the wife, face to face. Told her – look now, here it is; right here in front of me. I've turned the corner. I can feel it creaking in my bones, my teeth – the eyes are all cloudy in the mornings now. It's coming to get me, I swear.

Maybe ten good physical years left and that's it – tits up; roll over Beethoven. Ten years left to still throw a leg over a horse, like I used to; still fish waist-deep in a Western river; still sleep out in the open on flat ground under the starry canopy – like I used.

Pause, to himself:

When was that? This 'used to'. When *was* that?

Long pause. He stares out, then begins to stroll aimlessly, kicking at mounds of earth. He talks to the audience again.

(*Strolling.*) The kids had all flown the coop. Empty nesters – that's us, suddenly. Sitting around, folded up on sofas sipping tea and reading *The Week in Review* – the world going up in smoke across the blue Atlantic. Internecine warfare. Pathetic stuff. Truly. I proposed it to her gently, although she had no trouble seeing the sense of it, especially since my nervous condition had gone from bad to worse: constant pacing, talking to myself – which is no surprise – and sudden, unpredictable bursts of fury where I'd rip valuable objects of art off the walls and hurl them out the windows into the lush canyon of Park Avenue. Frederic Remingtons wrapped around the lamp posts, for instance. Charlie Russells purloined on bus-stop signs, crushed by maniacal yellow taxis. All stuff I'd discovered back in my truer days; hanging out worthless in remote Wyoming bars, skunk drunk in Silver Dollar saloons, staring bleary up at these masterful western murals nobody could recognise any more through the piled-up years of grime, tobacco juice and bar-room brawl blood. There they were – forgotten – just hanging dusty and crooked above the whisky.

'How much you want for that old cow painting up there?'

'That? Never thought about it. Why would you want to buy something like that?'

'Aw, just to hang up in the tack room, you know. Conversation piece.'

'Hell, I guess I'd take twenty bucks for it. Never look at the damn thing anyway, any more. My back's always facing it.'

'Twenty bucks? I'll take it.'

To audience.

Turned that twenty into a hundred grand; that hundred grand into a million. Whole thing just kinda snowballed. I raided every damn saloon, barn and attic west of the Missouri – north and south; took semi-loads of booty out of that country before anyone even began to take notice. Some of it's hanging in national museums now. What I couldn't see was how those old masterpieces would become like demons, trapping me in a life I wasn't meant for. Couldn't see that back then for hell or high water. Things come back to haunt you, that's for sure. Like my horse – this horse right here. I told the wife I'd been dreaming about my old horse, the one I'd left behind years before all this success with the paintings. I had one good one left, out in the Sand Hills on open range. Course he was just a colt back then. Big, good-looking son of a buck too. Kept visiting me night after night, just appearing in the dark, standing there with all his tack on – waiting – beckoning with his big brown eyes. I took it as some kind of a sign – some omen or other.

Sounds word.

OMEN.

Hobart moves back upstage towards the horse, staring down into the pit as he goes around it.

If I'd known how short he was going to last I'd have thought about it twice, that's for damn sure. Setting off into the Great Beyond with a doomed mount. Look at that. Dead. Can you believe it? There he is.

He kicks the horse again.

And now I've had to dig the gaping hole, of course. Can't just leave him out here to rot in the ragged wind. Let the coyotes strip him to ribbons. I'm not that callous. Horse served me well back in the day when work was work. Served me damn well. Been a good long while since I've dug a hole this big, by hand, by God. Back then, of course, I had a spine like a steel rod. Wind and muscle. Now – now it's like every pained shovelful is about to be your last. Every scoop. Pathetic. Got her done, anyhow. Got her good and done. Deep enough to keep the varmints from digging him back up. All that's left to do now is tip him in and fill it up. Time enough for that, I guess. All I got now is time.

He moves round to the upstage side of the horse and starts to struggle with the stiff front legs, trying to tip

*the horse up on its backbone so that it will topple
downstage into the pit. He alternately goes to the back
legs and does the same procedure, struggling with the
weight of the horse. Each time he pushes upward on
the legs they seem to stick a little higher in the air, very
stiff, and the horse slowly rotates on its spine. Hobart
keeps this up, going from front legs to back legs,
shoulder to hip, putting his whole body into it as he
continues to talk to himself.*

(*Struggling with the horse.*) This is somehow not at all
the way I'd envisioned it back in the planning stage; back
in the flush excitement of seeing myself setting out like
Lewis and Clark across the wild beyond. But maybe all
it ever is is blinded by the dreaming of what it might
become. Look what became of him – for example – one
of them – Lewis, wasn't it? Mr Meriwether – what was
he thinking? Shot himself with two pistols in some dark
slab-sided cabin on the Natchez Trace. A pistol to the
head and a pistol to the heart. What was he thinking?
To wind up like that after the greatest expedition in the
history of – Maybe he realised something. Maybe he did.
But me – not this – this is not what I foresaw for sure;
some dumb show – struggling with a dead horse,
mumbling to yourself in front of a gaping hole you've
spent a solid day digging; rambling on to imagined
faceless souls. There must be plenty out here, that's for
sure. Faceless. Not that I require an audience, God knows.
Don't get me wrong. I could just as easy keep it all silent,
I suppose, but just the sound of it keeps me company.
Voices.

   Stops, pauses, listens.

Some sense of company. There's got to be some sailing
spirits somewhere in all this space. The ones they left
behind. One or two at least – floating – gazing down in

dismay at this little sad display. There you are, rhyming again! Now you've caught yourself rhyming. Have you got no shame?

Pauses, out of breath.

This fucking horse.

Kicks horse; stares out at audience.

You wouldn't think a common saddle-horse could weigh as much as this.

He stares at the horse, which has now rotated almost to the halfway point on its spine, legs pointing stiffly in the air.

Of course, dead weight is famous for being heavier than live. All I need to do is tip him down into the hole there. Just tip him in. Easy enough to say.

Goes to edge of the pit, looks down.

Bound to be deep enough, don't you think?

Looks out at the audience.

I'm not climbing back down in there with the shovel, that's for sure. Can't help but feel you're digging your own damn tomb, with the damp walls growing higher and higher all around you, every shovelful. The smell too – the deeper you go. The history of it. The dinosaur. Bones. Ancient aching bones. The fossil fuels. All the shit that rolls through your numb skull as you shovel, one scoop at a time. You'd be surprised the way the mind can't sit still. Harking back. Leaping forward. Usually always back now, though. Rarely forward. Not with a dead horse and no prospects but hoofing out into the Lone Prairie for days on end.

Sounds words:

THE LONE PRAIRIE.

Pause. Listens.

What's it come to? What exactly did you have in mind?
Intentional exile? Pathetic stuff. What could you hope to
find? There's nothing out here. No one. Not a single
sorry soul. Look – just take a look.

*He holds the binoculars up and looks out, then lowers
them and stares at the audience.*

I've got to get this horse down in the hole. That's all I
know.

*He goes to the horse again, in a frenzy, trying to tip it
further up on its spine so that it might topple into the
pit. Horse inches to the midway point but won't budge
beyond it. Hobart rams his shoulder into the hip of the
horse, then the shoulder, but the horse remains firmly
on its spine, all four legs pointed stiffly to the sky.*

Fucking horse. Fucking goddamn horse.

Kicks it.

Look at that. Even dead he won't play ball. Stuck. Hung
up. What's the justice in it? I guess I could just leave him.
Just turn my back and leave him, belly up, hooves
pointed to the heavens. Walk away towards –

Stops, puts binoculars up again, scans horizon.

They must have been a desperate bunch, the pioneers.
Can you imagine?

Lowers binoculars.

All this – space. What were they thinking? Just movement. Migration. But me – what about me? I'd get out here, on my own, miles from nowhere, and somehow feel miraculously at peace? One with the wilderness? Suddenly, just from being here, I'd become what? What? Whole? After a whole life of being fractured, busted up, I'd suddenly become whole? The imagination's a terrible thing.

Pause.

Well, you can't very well go back now, can you? Tail between your legs. She'd laugh you right out of the house.

She? You're not going to tell me you're actually missing someone now, are you? The wife? The kids. The Mom. The Dead.

She was amazing to me. She was.

Was?

Is. Still. But then –

In the past?

Yes. In the past. She was beyond belief. I thought I'd died and gone to heaven. Oh, please – spare me.

She was –

What? Authentic, I suppose?

Beyond.

What's that? What's beyond authentic?

More – more than you can imagine.

Don't make me puke. You put yourself in this situation, now face the music.

I'm just saying –

What?

She –

You obviously can't explain her.

No.

You can't make do without her either. Is that it?

I thought I could. I had – in the past. I had been utterly alone – at other times. Completely. Without a soul. Not even family. So I knew what that was like. To some extent – but – I mean – I knew – I thought I could handle it. More or less. Complete aloneness. It didn't terrify me any more. Not like when you're little and – in the dark, listening – screams – distant – broken glass. Not like that – any more. You learn to make do. Make toast. Little fires. Sing a song to yourself. Hum a little. Still – I preferred being with her. Really. I did. It was nice. The companionship. Someone – something you could depend on. Take walks with. Have tea together. Coffee. Read the paper. Sleep with side by side. Touch and even – talk. Sometimes. Sex. Sometimes. Talk about whatever, although she loved politics. Liked to get excited about it. I despised it, so – that became – what – stale, I guess. Awkward after a while. But we got along. Don't get me wrong. For the most part. We became – tolerant, I guess. Of each other. Of each other's – what do you call them? Idiosyncrasies? Yes. Except for those occasional times when she'd explode and call me an asshole. Those were the moments I suddenly realised the depth of her anger. How much she deeply resented me. Surprising. Time together does that. Then we'd inevitably go silent. Sometimes days. A week and a half at most. But then – (*Sings.*) 'Together Again.' Back to the old routine. Everything forgotten. So, you can see how it became hard for me to imagine myself without her. What would I do? Where would I go? Who would I be with? Only myself again. Me and myself. Again. Why would I prefer that?

Snap out of it.

What? Sorry.

There's times I don't recognise you at all.

Like when?

Like now, for instance, I ask myself who is this person I blindly follow. Who's placed me in this precarious situation without any concern whatever for my welfare or safety. Who is this dangerous person?

Dangerous? (*Laughs.*)

You can laugh.

Have you thought about how you're going to get your ass out of here without a horse?

I've got beans enough. Beans enough for a week at least. Bacon. Jerky. Trail-mix. Plenty of water. I'm not worried.

Glad to see you were thinking ahead.

I'm well prepared for the worst.

You need to trim down.

What?

Trim. Cull. Get rid of this extra junk. How are you going to carry this out of here without a horse? Get rid of it.

Like what?

The saddle, for instance. Toss it down the hole.

The saddle? Bury the saddle?

The horse is dead.

True . . . But –

Toss it.

> *Hobart crosses to saddle, picks it up, drags it to the edge of the pit, hesitates, looks down into the hole.*

Just toss it. You'll get over it.

> *Hobart throws the saddle down into the pit. He looks after it, fondly.*

Now, the bridle.

> *He crosses to the bridle, picks it up, stares at it.*

Toss it.

> *He carries the bridle to the pit, throws it in, looks after it, fondly.*

Spurs.

> *He crosses to the spurs, picks them up, admires them.*

Hand-made Garcias. You can't find them any more.

What're you going to do? Hang them on your blank wall?

He carries the spurs to the pit, throws them in.

Good. Now – chaps.

He crosses to chaps, picks them up, carries them to the pit without much affection and throws them in.

Good. Now, hat.

No.

Toss it.

Not the hat.

Don't be a baby.

No. It won't get in the way.

Make a clean break.

From what?

You know.

Not the hat.

You're breaking my heart. Toss it.

Hobart crosses to hat, picks it up slowly, considers.

What about the sun?

It's setting.

Lights shift suddenly to a purple sunset, layered deep in the scrim.

What about rain and wind?

You can't predict it.

What about the whole idea?

Which one's that?

The West? The 'Wild Wild West'?

Sentimental claptrap.

Hobart crosses slowly to the pit with the hat held out
in front of him. He stops at the edge and looks down
into the hole, hanging on to the hat dearly.

I – can't.

Do it. Then what? There'll be nothing left.

The hat can't save you.

But –

What?

The history –

Gone.

No.

Gone.

Hobart suddenly flips the hat into the pit as though
afraid to hold on to it any longer. He turns and looks
directly at the audience, then looks back down the
hole, then back again to the audience.

(*To audience.*) I can't believe I just did that.

He looks back down into the hole.

There it is. I've done it now. Sunk. Separate. Completely
separated.

Stop your whimpering.

Hobart turns back towards the paraphernalia.

What else?

Blanket.

He crosses to the dark-green saddle-blanket, picks it up, turns towards the pit, stops, considers.

Don't be an idiot. You remember these nights out here. Ice on your eyelids waking up. Frosty toes. This is no country for the faint of heart.

He wraps the horse-blanket round his shoulders, crosses to the pit, looks down into it.

There it is. Down there. Gone. In a hole. Gone. Like dropping a bomb. You can't call it back. What a hat that was.

Can the melodrama.

There it is. Brand new Resistol. Quadruple X Beaver. A hat like that wasn't made to fall in a hole.

Just leave it. Turn away. Don't keep staring at it like some long-lost love.

Lost what?

Never mind. Just turn away.

Hobart turns his back on the hat, faces the audience, stares at them, blanket still wrapped round his shoulders.

(*To audience.*) This could really be it, now. To lose the hat. It's not a good sign. This could finally be it.

Suddenly the dead horse slams to the ground behind Hobart with a tremendous thud, accompanied by live bass timpani drum offstage, back to its starting position, falling towards upstage, away from audience, sending a huge cloud of dust up into the space. Hobart keeps staring directly at the audience, without turning upstage. Long pause as the dust slowly settles. Hobart slowly turns upstage to witness the disaster, blanket still round his shoulders.

Fucking horse. Goddamn.

He looks at the audience, then back to the horse. He moves cautiously upstage to the horse. Stops and stares at it. He gets closer and nudges it gently in the belly with his toe, then does it again.

(*To audience.*) Got a life of his own, that's for sure. That's what I always liked about the son-bitch; just when you thought he was finished he'd jump back up and rope six more steers for you and drag them all to the fire. Tougher than nails. Can't say as I blame him, though, for not wanting to go down in the damn hole. Makes you wonder, doesn't it? Maybe something's watching out for him; something hovering just above the hide – some guardian angel or other. More likely they'd be watching out for an innocent horse than a corrupted human. Don't get me wrong, superstition is not my cup of meat. Not to say that I haven't paid attention to it over the years – back when I worked for an honest living. Back in the days of AUTHENTICITY, when I rode for the brand, as they say: mending fences, doctoring calves, culling cows. Right here, as a matter of fact. Not too far. Out toward Blessing. Valentine. Up past the White River. 'Greasy Grass Country' is what the Ogallala used to call it. Crazy Horse was killed right near here, you know. Not too far. Right nearby. Bayoneted to death. Imagine that. Bayoneted.

Not unlike Christ when you come right down to it. Not to mention the two thieves. Spears to the ribs. Sacrificed like some wild beast. Some dangerous critter that might jump up out of the dark and rip your throat out for no reason. Tricked him into coming into the fort – starved him into it – promised him stuff – promised him land – hunting rights. Freedom – that's the worst of it. Freedom, they called it. They were full of promises back then. Still are. Same ones. Crazy Horse – A man of his people. Not many of them left.

Directly to audience.

Don't you think there ought to be a National Day of Rest for someone like that? A true American Hero. Close the schools. Close the post office. Five minutes of pure silence across the nation. Five minutes of pure silence.

Long pause. Hobart listens into the distance. He raises the binoculars to his eyes and scans the horizon. He sings as he scans.

Oh, didn't he ramble
Oh, didn't he ramble
Rambled all around
In and out of town.

Oh, didn't he ramble
Oh, didn't he ramble
He rambled 'til those butchers
Cut him down.

As Hobart starts singing the next verse, still scanning the horizon with binoculars to his eyes, a naked young woman emerges from deep in the pit, wearing Hobart's western hat and nothing else. He remains unaware of her as he continues singing and scanning. The young woman approaches him slowly and silently from behind,

takes the hat off and places it on Hobart's head.
Hobart pays no attention to the hat but continues
singing and scanning with the binoculars to his eyes.

He rambled in a gambling game
He rambled on the green
The gamblers there showed him a trick
That he had never seen.

He lost his roll and jewellery
He like to lost his life
He lost the car that carried him there
And somebody stole his wife.

Through the last verse, the young woman returns
silently to the pit, descends slowly, and disappears.
Completely unaware of her presence, Hobart continues
singing and scanning.

Oh, didn't he ramble
Oh, didn't he ramble
Rambled all around
In and out of town.

Oh, didn't he ramble
Oh, didn't he ramble
He rambled 'til those butchers
Cut him down.

Hobart stops singing, lowers binoculars, stares straight
at the audience, never having seen the young woman.
Pause. He reaches up and feels the hat on his head,
takes it off and stares at it. Stares at audience, stares
at hat again, then turns and stares down at the pit.
He turns back, stares at the audience, looks at the hat,
looks at the pit again, looks at the audience. He looks
at the pit, then walks over to the pit and stares down
into it. He looks at the audience, looks at the pit, looks

at the hat. Pause, then he tosses the hat back down into the pit and stares down after it, fondly. Pause. He looks at audience.

(*To audience.*) I can't believe I did that again. This is getting dire. This is getting dark and dire.

Lights shift abruptly to dusk. Hobart looks up at the darkening sky.

I've got to get this horse in the ground. How am I going to get this horse in the ground?

He starts towards stage right, looking for his rope.

Just leave him.

He stops abruptly. Considers.

What?

Leave the horse.

I can't just walk away.

He goes again for the rope.

He's dead.

I owe it to him.

Hobart finds the coil of rope, picks it up and builds a loop. He starts upstage for the horse with the rope in his hand. He stops again. Listens.

You've got to find your way out of here. Find your way back to the road. Where exactly did you park the horse-trailer? Can you remember that much?

Puts binoculars to eyes, scans horizon.

I CAN'T SEE THE ROAD.

It's going to be dark-thirty before you know it.

He panics.

I can't see the road!

Lowers binoculars, stares out.

You better build a fire.

Goes towards the horse again.

No! I'm not spending the night out here, if that's what you think. Are you nuts?

I thought you were self-sufficient. Isn't that what you led me to believe? Entirely on your own. Independent?

Where did we park the horse-trailer? Can't you remember?

We?

Me. Us.

How should I know? You were the one got carried away. 'Right here!' you said. 'Right here! This is perfect! Pull over.'

It *was* perfect. The day. The place. No one around. The sky.

Then why can't you remember?

I got excited, I guess.

Excited?

Yes.

Like a little boy?

No.

Like a little girl?

Don't be insulting! I got excited about finally taking off into it. About getting here. About –

What?

The Great Beyond!

Why do you always exaggerate?

It was way better than I imagined. For once. More incredible. The sky. The flat buttes. The distance. Crows.

Then why in the world did you feed him a nosebag full of oats, of all things? Right at the start.

I wanted to – fire him up. Make sure he had enough energy for the ordeal.

You fired him up all right.

I didn't know he was going to suck it down his lung. How was I supposed to know that?

You've lost your touch. There was a time you would have known better.

Stop badgering me! What's done is done. I'm going to get this horse in the ground and move on. I'm not camping here overnight, that's for sure.

He gets to the horse, loops the rope around both front feet, carrying on a dialogue with himself as he works.

You've grown soft.

What?

Soft. You're in a panic now.

I'm not at all.

Then why the sudden frenzy?

He goes to the hind feet and wraps another loop around them.

It's time to move on. You said that yourself.

Pause. Hobart is breathing hard from the work.

She'd be fixing supper for you about now, wouldn't she?

He stops working with the rope, looks out.

She?

She'd be fixing things up, making things cosy. Lighting the lamps.

He goes back to work, wrapping the rope around the horse's legs and tugging it snug.

Stop this constant goading! What're you trying to do to me?

I'm on your side.

No, you're not. You never were. You've lied to me about everything. You're a traitor!

You've lost your nerve, is what it is. If you ever had any to begin with.

This was not about bravado.

No?

Absolutely not! I've got nothing to prove.

No?

Stop taunting me! I'm trying to get this done.

She'd be sitting by the fire, probably; listening to the radio, reading the paper, sipping English tea.

She only reads the paper in the morning.

Maybe she's gone by now. Did you ever think of that? Long gone.

He stops working abruptly.

What?

Maybe she's not even there any more. Moved on to another life.

No, don't say that.

Why not? What's to keep her? *You're* not there.

She'll be there.

You never said you were coming back.

I never said I wasn't.

Maybe she's run off with another man. A better man.

Stop it! I didn't come all the way out here to be tortured!

Hobart returns to struggling with the rope. He hauls the loose rope downstage centre, in front of the pit, the two ends attached to the horse's front and back legs. He starts pulling and tugging on the rope, trying to rotate the horse up on its back again, as before.

Slowly, the carcass begins to co-operate.

(*Tugging on rope.*) Why doesn't this fucking horse want to go down in the hole!

Maybe he's not entirely dead.

He stops pulling. Asks himself:

What?

Maybe there's still some life left in him. Why else would he be resisting?

Pause. Hobart looks at the horse. Looks at the audience. He runs upstage to the horse. Looks at it. Looks at the audience. Looks at the horse. Gives the horse a tremendous kick in the belly.

He's dead! He's completely dead.

Leave him, then. Just leave him behind.

No! I already told you. It's out of the question.

Hobart runs back downstage, picks up the loose rope and starts hauling on it again, the horse very gradually rotating on its spine.

(*Hauling on the rope.*) Maybe it's true – Maybe I didn't think it all the way through. Maybe I couldn't actually foresee what it was going to be like. But I'm not leaving this old horse out here in the wind and sun to rot away like some forgotten road-kill. He deserves better than that.

Your loyalty is very touching.

Don't patronise me.

No, it is. I'm deeply touched. I truly am. I had no idea you were capable of such kindness.

What's that supposed to mean? I'm not a cruel person. Not cruel by nature, anyway. I'd never intentionally hurt a soul.

You keep kicking your horse.

HE'S DEAD! HE'S FUCKING DEAD!

He throws down the rope, runs back upstage to the horse and starts savagely kicking it repeatedly as he rants on.

(*Kicking horse in rage.*) See? See that? Doesn't feel a thing. Doesn't feel a goddamn thing! I can kick him in the head and he wouldn't feel it.

Kicks horse in head.

See? Like a block of stone. I can kick him in the neck.

Kicks horse in neck.

I can pull his tail. Watch.

He runs to the horse's tail and yanks on it viciously.

Watch this. See this? I can kick him right in the ass and he won't feel it. You see?

Kicks horse in the ass.

See that? He doesn't even blink. I could kick him in the balls if he had any. I'd kick him in his fucking – I'd kick him from here to –

Series of kicks all over the horse's body.

I'd kick him and kick him and kick him – and kick him and –

*Hobart collapses in a heap on the horse's belly,
exhausted from his outburst. Slowly, he begins to weep
softly, head tucked into his elbow. Long pause as he
grieves. His arm slowly embraces the horse's belly. He
pats horse softly, strokes its belly. He keeps his head
down, sobbing softly. After a while, distant thunder is
heard, followed by branches of lightning on the horizon.
Hobart looks up slowly at sky.*

(*To himself.*) So, this is the way you wind up – not like
some gallant bushwhacker but flattened out babbling in
the open plains. What the hell did you have in mind
anyway? What was it?

He pats the horse, talks to it.

Maybe the two of us – huh? Maybe that's it. Both of us
were meant to go down in the hole. Do you think so?
Maybe that's exactly it. Both of us. Should've dug it
deeper.

*He props himself up on his elbows on the horse's belly,
talks to the horse.*

If I was to jump down in there with you, would you be
a little more co-operative? Would you maybe be less
lonely? Is that it? Just the plain old lonesomeness of it?

*He stands and stares down at the horse. More thunder
and lightning in the distance. He looks out, then
speaks to horse again.*

I don't expect an answer right away.

You can take your time to consider. Just know that at this
point – this particular low moment in time – I *am* willing
to take the leap. I've got nothing to lose.

Pause.

But I'm not jumping down in there if you chicken out on me. I'm not diving down into all that infernal blackness without getting some assurance that I'll have company.

Pause.

Company – some – warmth.

Thunder and lightning again. Hobart looks at the sky.

What're we going to do? Huh? Just lay out here and get rained on like a couple of rocks? Drenched to the teeth. You expect me to just hang around here and get rained on while you play dead?

Pause, stares at horse.

No. No, I'm not making any deals. No deals. I'm not bargaining with a dead horse.

He moves downstage right to the remaining equipment, talking as he goes. He searches through the duffle, pulls out a flashlight, switches it on; finds a very small white canvas tent and starts trying to set it up in the semi-darkness. Intermittent thunder and lightning. He talks continuously.

(*Trying to set up the tent.*) Just because *you've* decided to cash in your chips is no reason for me to just –

Turns to horse violently.

I'm not talking to you any more, all right? I'm not buying into this. This is not my first county fair, you know. I can make it through this. I've been through some bitter squalls in my time. Hail the size of baseballs. Freezing rain. Wind that would knock your dick in the dirt, knock you right out of the saddle. This –

Waves at darkening sky.

This is nothing.

*The tent collapses. He repeats trying to set it up as he
rants on.*

This is – this is some little passing gully-wash. Some piss
in the ocean. Not enough to turn the dust to mud. I've
got beans here. Plenty of beans! Bacon! I've got jerky!
Trail-mix! Shelter! What else do you need? What else?

The tent collapses again. He soldiers on.

A little fortitude maybe. Nothing more. Piece of cake.
You don't think I've just stumbled out here like some
greenhorn tourist, do you? Some SUV nincompoop!

Thunder and lightning closer.

I cut my teeth on this kind of country. Worse! Broke
boulders in the High Sierras. Crushed primitive elements!
Squashed snakes and scorpions. Right here. I'm not just
some bumbling fool looking for a handout. Look at these
hands! You see these!

Holds his hands up for the horse to see.

Look at these hands!

The tent collapses again. He tries again to set it up.

You don't earn hands like these backing down from
Manifest Destiny! No, sir. Not a bit of it.

To the horse, as he struggles with tent:

You, now – *you* might belong to that tribe of weaklings
who's ready to roll over and play dead in the midst of

monumental challenge, but some of us – some of us are
aware of our –

The tent collapses again.

Fucking tent!

*Loud thunder and lightning close by. Hobart becomes
more frantic in his tent assembly.*

(*Struggling with the tent.*) What's with this tent? This isn't
my original tent, is it? Who ordered this fucking tent?
Why is it nothing's co-operating? I shouldn't be having
this much trouble with – I don't understand it.

*Throughout the next sequence the storm becomes
more violent, finally reaching a crescendo as Hobart
succeeds in getting the tent to stay up.*

I do not understand why I'm having so much trouble
taming the Wild. I've done this already. Haven't I already
been through all this? We closed the frontier in 1890-
something, didn't we? Didn't we already accomplish
that? The Iron Horse – coast to coast. Blasted all the
buffalo out of here. An ocean of bones from sea to shining
sea. Chased the heathen Redman down to Florida. Trails
of tears. Paid the Niggers off in mules and rich black dirt.
Whupped the Chinese and strung them up with their own
damn ponytails. Decapitated the Mexicans. Erected steel
walls. Sucked these hills barren of gold. Ripped the top
soil as far as the eye can see. Dammed up all the rivers
and flooded the valleys for recreational purposes. Run
off the small farmers. Destroyed education. Turned our
children into criminals. Demolished art. Invaded
sovereign nations. What else can we possibly do?

*Finally Hobart gets the tent set up. He climbs inside
with the flashlight on. There's barely enough room for*

*him. He hunkers down facing the audience through
the open flap of the tent, knees tucked up under his
chin, arms wrapped round his lower legs. Panting and
grasping for air from his tirade, he stares out. Thunder
and lightning crescendo. The lightning silhouettes the
dead horse with its legs sticking straight up. Hobart's
flashlight illuminates tent. Sound of deluge. Weather
begins to subside into distance, enough for Hobart's
plea to be heard from tent. Darkness pervades.*

(*Breathing hard, trying to get his wind back inside the
tent.*) If I were going to pray –

You?

'*If*,' I said. 'If.'

Don't make me puke. The going gets a little tough and
suddenly you're a man of the cloth?

Not that. No.

An epiphany, is it?

'*If*'! Is there anything wrong with 'if'?

What would you pray for?

A sunny day. One last, bright, shining, sunny day. Is that
too much to ask?

What makes you think you deserve it?

Well, there have been other sunny days I never deserved.
Gratuitous sunny days where I woke up and they just
happened to be there. Beams of light streaming through
the window. Her golden hair –

(*Mocking.*) 'Her golden hair.'

Don't make fun of me! I can't take it! I'm feeling very –

You're a mess. You're an absolute mess.

Pause. The weather has settled into the distance, but the light stays subdued.

So, this is it, I guess, huh? 'Prominent New York Art Dealer Found Dead in Badlands with Dead Horse. There were no apparent signs of a struggle.'

Pathetic.

Do you think she'll attend the funeral?

She?

You know who I mean.

Don't ask me personal questions. It's too late for that. Way too late.

Why are you such a bitter enemy?

We don't have much in common. Do we?

No, I guess not.

You never went out of your way to see my side of things.

No, it's true.

Then why are you so surprised?

I just thought maybe –

Maybe what?

Maybe you'd grow tired of it.

Me? It takes two to tango.

44

Long pause.

What do you suppose I had in mind?

'Authenticity', wasn't it? 'AUTHENTICITY'.

Oh. Yeah.

It's only an idea.

Yeah.

Only a passing thought, like all the rest. Marching on.

True.

Pause.

Do you think she'll forgive me?

Sooner or later. Maybe not.

Pause.

I think I'm going to try it.

What?

Praying.

By all means. Be my guest.

I've never actually tried it, have you?

Once. It didn't work.

You – put your hands together?

I think it's optional.

Close your eyes?

Why not.

Think – what? Think of God?

Suit yourself.

I don't think I can think of God.

Then dream something up.

A bright – shining – sunny – day.

That'll work.

Slowly, scrim begins to brighten, darkness recedes, thunder and lightning are gone. Morning light fills the stage. Hobart slowly emerges from the tent, leaving the flashlight behind. He walks downstage centre, looks up at the sky, then turns upstage and looks at the horse, which is still in its rigid, belly-up position. He walks to the edge of the pit and looks down into it. He sees his hat in the hole. He runs his hand over the top of his head. He turns to the audience. Speaks directly to them:

Hat like that shouldn't be down in a hole. Brand new hat. Hardly even got a chance to break it in.

He looks down at the hat again, then crosses to the side of the pit where he originally made his entrance and climbs back down into the hole, disappearing.

Long pause, then the dead horse slams forward, downstage, again with a mighty boom accompanied by bass timpani offstage, dust rising all around, but the hole is not quite wide enough to accommodate the entire horse. His legs from the hocks and knees down hang up on the downstage lip of the stage and the horse's body ends up straddling the pit. Pause, as dust

begins to settle, then Hobart's voice is heard singing
from deep in the pit as the lights begin slowly to fade.

Oh, didn't he ramble
Oh, didn't he ramble
He rambled all around
In and out of town.

Oh, didn't he ramble
Oh, didn't he ramble
He rambled 'til those butchers
Cut him down.

Lights to black. Dr John music from opening back in
as the lights rise for the curtain call.

End.